catalphabet

KATHLEEN LEEMON SWARTZ

ISBN: 1-4392-1150-7
ISBN-13: 9781439211502

Visit www.booksurge.com to order additional copies.

Dagger toes and serpent tail
Whiskered nose on mouse's trail
Silken fur and sandy tongue
Feline antics keep you young.

THIS BOOK IS DEDICATED TO

Tiger

Fred

Mister Mistopheles

Macavity

K.C.

Spook

my Lizzie

&

every other cat
who has deigned to accept
my attention and my admiration.

A is for **attitude** –
cats are aloof.

B is for **bathing** –
Would you like proof?

C is for **claws**,
sharp as daggers,

that's clear.

D is for **daring** –
this cat
shows
no fear.

E is for **energy**!
Look at this leap!

F is for **fur** in your face

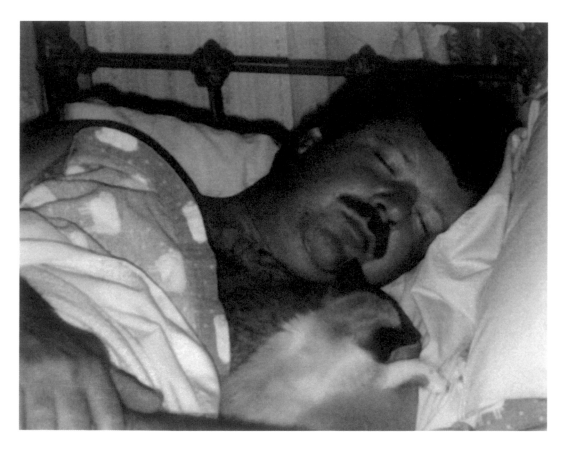

while you sleep.

 is for **gentle** – which often they are, but . . .

H is
a **hiss**
that says

Don't come too far!

I is for **innocent**.

Such a sweet face!

J is I'm *just* keeping all in its place.

K is for **kittens** who capture your heart.

L is for **lonely** when

you have to part.

M is for **mice** that
cats love to pursue.

N is for nesting.

Most places will do.

O is for **outlaw**, won't come when he should.

P is for **purrs** that declare life is good!

Q is for **quiet**.

She's sometimes serene.

R is for **regal** because she's a queen.

S is for stretching,

D
E
L
I
C
I
O
U
S
L
Y

slow.

T is a **tree-top** perch.

Look out below!

U is for **under** the cap on the couch.

V is for **velvety** felines that crouch.

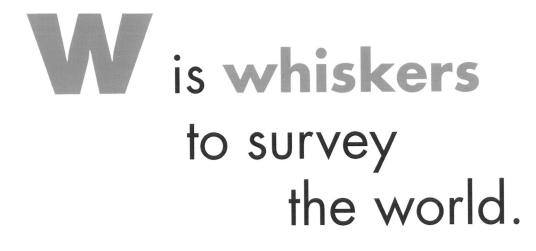

W is **whiskers**
to survey
the world.

X marks the spot
where the tabby
is curled.

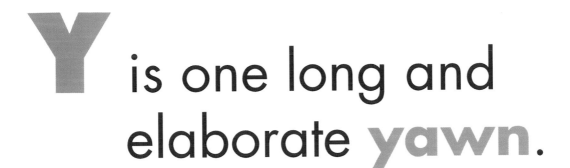

Y is one long and elaborate **yawn**.

Z is for

Zip up this bag
and we're gone!

FEATURED FELINES AND THEIR STAFFS:

Cover – Jerry, Tom, and Too – Tom and Cathy Eash
A – Mister Mistopheles and Macavity – K. L. Swartz
B – Boogie – the Spangler Family
C – Tom and Too – Tom and Cathy Eash
D – Lizzie – KLS
E – K.C. – Kim Swartz
F – K.C. and Dave Swartz
G – Snowball and Marshmallow – Lorna Wilson
H – Mickey – the Spangler Family
I – Bobbie – Tom and Cathy Eash
J – Clarence – Judy Darr
K – Sweetypie and Boots – Tom and Cathy Eash
L – Fred [a.k.a. Madeline] – Bill Leemon
M – Lizzie – KLS
N – Mister – KLS, and Thomas - Jeanne Andersen
O – Thomas Edison – Jeanne Andersen
P – Smokey – Eric and Michelle Risser
Q – Minnie – the Spangler Family
R – Missie – the Spangler Family
S – Puddy – Tom and Cathy Eash
T – Tom Edison and Benjamin Franklin – Jeanne Andersen
U - Whiskers - Buchanan Carpenter
V – Willie – Ruth Leemon Hoppus
W – Tippy – Tom and Cathy Eash
X – Cooper – Roberta Markley
Y - Whiskers - Buchanan Carpenter
Z – Tom – Tom and Cathy Eash

With appreciation and apologies to those felines whose photos were submitted but unused.

Kathleen Leemon Swartz is a Hoosier *born and raised* who has attended school every year of her life since the age of five – first as a student, and then as an elementary teacher, administrator, and teacher again.

As a lover of reading, poetry, words, and cats, she started this book while developing a book writing project for her fifth grade students. Much appreciation goes to one of those students, Kristin Duff. Having no cat photos of her own, she borrowed from friends and neighbors and was responsible for many of the pictures included in *catalphabet*.

Enormous appreciation is also due to Mr. Tom Eash, without whose technological expertise none of the pictures would have been in acceptable form for publishing!

Watch for other titles by Swartz - *Every Family Has One,* and *Fall in Indiana.* Her next goal is to complete a book in progress on the life of Oliver H. P. T. Morton, Indiana's civil war governor.

2385184